# DO THAT WHICH YOU ARE MOST AFRAID OF...

SKETA

---

DAILY ACTION AT YOUR CRAFT, BRINGS YOU CLOSER TO PERFECTION.

SKETA

## Focus is Everything!

---

CARIN
WORLD
RESPO

---

# LIFE ROCKS!

...Sketa

---

# ROME WASN'T BUILT IN A DAY, BUT IT WAS BUILT!

SKETA

---

*Build y*
*realit*

---

# CHANGE NEEDS CHANGE.

...SKETA

---

## Focus is Everything!

IF YOU CAN BEAT 'EM, JOIN 'EM; UNTIL AN OPPORTUNITY ARISES, WHEREBY YOU CAN TOSS 'EM.

...SKETA

---

IF YOU HA
JUST O

YOU H
DIF

R OUR
YONE'S
LITY.

DOWNTIME
IS
EVERYTHING!
...SKETA

CHANGE NEEDS
CHANGE.
...SKETA

Focus is
Everything!

reams a
ive in.

SUCCESS
=
HOW MUCH YOU WANT IT
+
HOW HARD YOU WILL WORK
TO GET IT!
...SKETA

LIFE
ROCKS!
...Sketa

PROVED,
RSON'S

Focus is
Everything!

ADE A
CE.

EVERYDAY IS
A BLESSED
DAY.
...SKETA

LIVE A LIFE,
NOT AN
EXISTENCE.
...SKETA

# DO THAT WHICH YOU ARE MOST AFRAID OF...

SKETA

DAILY ACTION AT YOUR CRAFT, BRINGS YOU CLOSER TO PERFECTION.

SKETA

# Focus is Everything!

CARI
WORLD
RESPO

# LIFE ROCKS!

...Sketa

# ROME WASN'T BUILT IN A DAY, BUT IT WAS BUILT!

SKETA

Build y
realit

# CHANGE NEEDS CHANGE.

...SKETA

# Focus is Everything!

IF YOU CAN BEAT 'EM, JOIN 'EM; UNTIL AN OPPORTUNITY ARISES, WHEREBY YOU CAN TOSS 'EM.

...SKETA

IF YOU HA
JUST O

YOU H
DIF

OUR
YONE'S
ITY.

DOWNTIME
IS
EVERYTHING!
...SKETA

CHANGE NEEDS
CHANGE.
...SKETA

Focus is
Everything!

SUCCESS
=
HOW MUCH YOU WANT IT
+
HOW HARD YOU WILL WORK
TO GET IT!
...SKETA

eams a
ve in.

LIFE
ROCKS!
...Sketa

PROVED,
SON'S

ADE A
CE.

Focus is
Everything!

EVERYDAY IS
A BLESSED
DAY.
...SKETA

LIVE A LIFE,
NOT AN
EXISTENCE.
...SKETA

# LLWf™
## EST.2014

>LLWF<

Live Life Without Fear

is dedicated to
my late father who sadly
passed away from cancer, in
2014.

Like so many, his time was cut
short, but he lived, loved, and
laughed like no other I have
known.

Through his inspiration and my
creation, I pray I have honoured
his life and helped a million other
individuals to:

Live Life Without Fear

...as he continues to remind me
every day.

# LILIWIOFE'
## Live Life Without Fear

LIFE DIARY

Published in Australia by
**ELK PUBLISHING**

**2020** © SKETA

PERSONAL INFORMATION

NAME

ADDRESS

MOBILE

E-MAIL

BUSINESS NAME

BUSINESS ADDRESS

BUSINESS PHONE

BUSINESS E-MAIL

BUEINESS WEBSITE

DRIVERS LICENCE

In case of accident please contact:
NAME

ADDRESS

PHONE

LLWF: Live Life Without Fear Diaries are specifically designed to motivate, inspire, energise, organise and realise that you can achieve so much more than you think you can and that you don't need to be afraid to ask the universe for your place among the stars.

**LLWF: Live Life Without Fear**

Published in Australia
by ELK Publishing

LLWf™
EST.2014

# 2021 Planner

| JANUARY | FEBRUARY | MARCH |
|---|---|---|
| 1 _____ | 1 _____ | 1 _____ |
| 2 _____ | 2 _____ | 2 _____ |
| 3 _____ | 3 _____ | 3 _____ |
| 4 _____ | 4 _____ | 4 _____ |
| 5 _____ | 5 _____ | 5 _____ |
| 6 _____ | 6 _____ | 6 _____ |
| 7 _____ | 7 _____ | 7 _____ |
| 8 _____ | 8 _____ | 8 _____ |
| 9 _____ | 9 _____ | 9 _____ |
| 10 _____ | 10 _____ | 10 _____ |
| 11 _____ | 11 _____ | 11 _____ |
| 12 _____ | 12 _____ | 12 _____ |
| 13 _____ | 13 _____ | 13 _____ |
| 14 _____ | 14 _____ | 14 _____ |
| 15 _____ | 15 _____ | 15 _____ |
| 16 _____ | 16 _____ | 16 _____ |
| 17 _____ | 17 _____ | 17 _____ |
| 18 _____ | 18 _____ | 18 _____ |
| 19 _____ | 19 _____ | 19 _____ |
| 20 _____ | 20 _____ | 20 _____ |
| 21 _____ | 21 _____ | 21 _____ |
| 22 _____ | 22 _____ | 22 _____ |
| 23 _____ | 23 _____ | 23 _____ |
| 24 _____ | 24 _____ | 24 _____ |
| 25 _____ | 25 _____ | 25 _____ |
| 26 _____ | 26 _____ | 26 _____ |
| 27 _____ | 27 _____ | 27 _____ |
| 28 _____ | 28 _____ | 28 _____ |
| 29 _____ | 29 _____ | 29 _____ |
| 30 _____ | | 30 _____ |
| 31 _____ | | 31 _____ |

| APRIL | MAY | JUNE |
|-------|-----|------|

| APRIL | MAY | JUNE |
|-------|-----|------|
| 1 _____ | 1 _____ | 1 _____ |
| 2 _____ | 2 _____ | 2 _____ |
| 3 _____ | 3 _____ | 3 _____ |
| 4 _____ | 4 _____ | 4 _____ |
| 5 _____ | 5 _____ | 5 _____ |
| 6 _____ | 6 _____ | 6 _____ |
| 7 _____ | 7 _____ | 7 _____ |
| 8 _____ | 8 _____ | 8 _____ |
| 9 _____ | 9 _____ | 9 _____ |
| 10_____ | 10_____ | 10_____ |
| 11_____ | 11_____ | 11_____ |
| 12_____ | 12_____ | 12_____ |
| 13_____ | 13_____ | 13_____ |
| 14_____ | 14_____ | 14_____ |
| 15_____ | 15_____ | 15_____ |
| 16_____ | 16_____ | 16_____ |
| 17_____ | 17_____ | 17_____ |
| 18_____ | 18_____ | 18_____ |
| 19_____ | 19_____ | 19_____ |
| 20_____ | 20_____ | 20_____ |
| 21_____ | 21_____ | 21_____ |
| 22_____ | 22_____ | 22_____ |
| 23_____ | 23_____ | 23_____ |
| 24_____ | 24_____ | 24_____ |
| 25_____ | 25_____ | 25_____ |
| 26_____ | 26_____ | 26_____ |
| 27_____ | 27_____ | 27_____ |
| 28_____ | 28_____ | 28_____ |
| 29_____ | 29_____ | 29_____ |
| 30_____ | 30_____ | 30_____ |
|  | 31_____ |  |

| APRIL | MAY | JUNE |
|-------|-----|------|

# 2021 Planner

| JULY | AUGUST | SEPTEMBER |
|------|--------|-----------|

| JULY | AUGUST | SEPTEMBER |
|------|--------|-----------|
| 1 | 1 | 1 |
| 2 | 2 | 2 |
| 3 | 3 | 3 |
| 4 | 4 | 4 |
| 5 | 5 | 5 |
| 6 | 6 | 6 |
| 7 | 7 | 7 |
| 8 | 8 | 8 |
| 9 | 9 | 9 |
| 10 | 10 | 10 |
| 11 | 11 | 11 |
| 12 | 12 | 12 |
| 13 | 13 | 13 |
| 14 | 14 | 14 |
| 15 | 15 | 15 |
| 16 | 16 | 16 |
| 17 | 17 | 17 |
| 18 | 18 | 18 |
| 19 | 19 | 19 |
| 20 | 20 | 20 |
| 21 | 21 | 21 |
| 22 | 22 | 22 |
| 23 | 23 | 23 |
| 24 | 24 | 24 |
| 25 | 25 | 25 |
| 26 | 26 | 26 |
| 27 | 27 | 27 |
| 28 | 28 | 28 |
| 29 | 29 | 29 |
| 30 | 30 | 30 |
| 31 | 31 | |

| JULY | AUGUST | SEPTEMBER |
|------|--------|-----------|

| OCTOBER | NOVEMBER | DECEMBER |
|---|---|---|

| OCTOBER | NOVEMBER | DECEMBER |
|---|---|---|

1 _____ 1 _____ 1 _____
2 _____ 2 _____ 2 _____
3 _____ 3 _____ 3 _____
4 _____ 4 _____ 4 _____
5 _____ 5 _____ 5 _____
6 _____ 6 _____ 6 _____
7 _____ 7 _____ 7 _____
8 _____ 8 _____ 8 _____
9 _____ 9 _____ 9 _____
10_____ 10_____ 10_____
11_____ 11_____ 11_____
12_____ 12_____ 12_____
13_____ 13_____ 13_____
14_____ 14_____ 14_____
15_____ 15_____ 15_____
16_____ 16_____ 16_____
17_____ 17_____ 17_____
18_____ 18_____ 18_____
19_____ 19_____ 19_____
20_____ 20_____ 20_____
21_____ 21_____ 21_____
22_____ 22_____ 22_____
23_____ 23_____ 23_____
24_____ 24_____ 24_____
25_____ 25_____ 25_____
26_____ 26_____ 26_____
27_____ 27_____ 27_____
28_____ 28_____ 28_____
29_____ 29_____ 29_____
30_____ 30_____ 30_____
31_____

# 2021 CALENDAR

## JANUARY

| M | T | W | T | F | S | S |
|---|---|---|---|---|---|---|
|   |   |   |   | 1 | 2 | 3 |
| 4 | 5 | 6 | 7 | 8 | 9 | 10 |
| 11 | 12 | 13 | 14 | 15 | 16 | 17 |
| 18 | 19 | 20 | 21 | 22 | 23 | 24 |
| 25 | 26 | 27 | 28 | 29 | 30 | 31 |

## FEBRUARY

| M | T | W | T | F | S | S |
|---|---|---|---|---|---|---|
| 1 | 2 | 3 | 4 | 5 | 6 | 7 |
| 8 | 9 | 10 | 11 | 12 | 13 | 14 |
| 15 | 16 | 17 | 18 | 19 | 20 | 21 |
| 22 | 23 | 24 | 25 | 26 | 27 | 28 |
|   |   |   |   |   |   |   |

## MARCH

| M | T | W | T | F | S | S |
|---|---|---|---|---|---|---|
| 1 | 2 | 3 | 4 | 5 | 6 | 7 |
| 8 | 9 | 10 | 11 | 12 | 13 | 14 |
| 15 | 16 | 17 | 18 | 19 | 20 | 21 |
| 22 | 23 | 24 | 25 | 26 | 27 | 28 |
| 29 | 30 | 31 |   |   |   |   |

## APRIL

| M | T | W | T | F | S | S |
|---|---|---|---|---|---|---|
|   |   |   | 1 | 2 | 3 | 4 |
| 5 | 6 | 7 | 8 | 9 | 10 | 11 |
| 12 | 13 | 14 | 15 | 16 | 17 | 18 |
| 19 | 20 | 21 | 22 | 23 | 24 | 25 |
| 26 | 27 | 28 | 29 | 30 |   |   |

## MAY

| M | T | W | T | F | S | S |
|---|---|---|---|---|---|---|
| 31 |   |   |   |   | 1 | 2 |
| 3 | 4 | 5 | 6 | 7 | 8 | 9 |
| 10 | 11 | 12 | 13 | 14 | 15 | 16 |
| 17 | 18 | 19 | 20 | 21 | 22 | 23 |
| 24 | 25 | 26 | 27 | 28 | 29 | 30 |

## JUNE

| M | T | W | T | F | S | S |
|---|---|---|---|---|---|---|
|   | 1 | 2 | 3 | 4 | 5 | 6 |
| 7 | 8 | 9 | 10 | 11 | 12 | 13 |
| 14 | 15 | 16 | 17 | 18 | 19 | 20 |
| 21 | 22 | 23 | 24 | 25 | 26 | 27 |
| 28 | 29 | 30 |   |   |   |   |

# 2021 CALENDAR

## JULY

| M | T | W | T | F | S | S |
|---|---|---|---|---|---|---|
|   |   |   | 1 | 2 | 3 | 4 |
| 5 | 6 | 7 | 8 | 9 | 10 | 11 |
| 12 | 13 | 14 | 15 | 16 | 17 | 18 |
| 19 | 20 | 21 | 22 | 23 | 24 | 25 |
| 26 | 27 | 28 | 29 | 30 | 31 |   |

## AUGUST

| M | T | W | T | F | S | S |
|---|---|---|---|---|---|---|
| 30 | 31 |   |   |   |   | 1 |
| 2 | 3 | 4 | 5 | 6 | 7 | 8 |
| 9 | 10 | 11 | 12 | 13 | 14 | 15 |
| 16 | 17 | 18 | 19 | 20 | 21 | 22 |
| 23 | 24 | 25 | 26 | 27 | 28 | 29 |

## SEPTEMBER

| M | T | W | T | F | S | S |
|---|---|---|---|---|---|---|
|   |   | 1 | 2 | 3 | 4 | 5 |
| 6 | 7 | 8 | 9 | 10 | 11 | 12 |
| 13 | 14 | 15 | 16 | 17 | 18 | 19 |
| 20 | 21 | 22 | 23 | 24 | 25 | 26 |
| 27 | 28 | 29 | 30 |   |   |   |

## OCTOBER

| M | T | W | T | F | S | S |
|---|---|---|---|---|---|---|
|   |   |   |   | 1 | 2 | 3 |
| 4 | 5 | 6 | 7 | 8 | 9 | 10 |
| 11 | 12 | 13 | 14 | 15 | 16 | 17 |
| 18 | 19 | 20 | 21 | 22 | 23 | 24 |
| 25 | 26 | 27 | 28 | 29 | 30 | 31 |

## NOVEMBER

| M | T | W | T | F | S | S |
|---|---|---|---|---|---|---|
| 1 | 2 | 3 | 4 | 5 | 6 | 7 |
| 8 | 9 | 10 | 11 | 12 | 13 | 14 |
| 15 | 16 | 17 | 18 | 19 | 20 | 21 |
| 22 | 23 | 24 | 25 | 26 | 27 | 28 |
| 29 | 30 |   |   |   |   |   |

## DECEMBER

| M | T | W | T | F | S | S |
|---|---|---|---|---|---|---|
|   |   | 1 | 2 | 3 | 4 | 5 |
| 6 | 7 | 8 | 9 | 10 | 11 | 12 |
| 13 | 14 | 15 | 16 | 17 | 18 | 19 |
| 20 | 21 | 22 | 23 | 24 | 25 | 26 |
| 27 | 28 | 29 | 30 | 31 |   |   |

# PUBLIC HOLIDAYS 2021

**WORLD OBSERVATIONS**
Jan 1 - New Year's Day
Dec 25 - Christmas Day
Dec 26 - Boxing Day
Dec 27 - Christmas Day Holiday

**AUSTRALIA**
Jan 26 - Australian Day
Jan 26 - Australia Day Holiday
Mar 9 - Labour Day
Apr 2 - Good Friday
Apr 3 - Easter Saturday
Apr 4 - Easter Sunday
Apr 5 - Easter Monday
April 25 - Anzac Day
Jun 8 - Queens Birthday Holiday (Oct 4 - Qld only)
Dec 28 - Boxing Day Holiday

**NEW ZEALAND**
Feb 1 - Auckland Anniversary
Feb 8 - Waitangi Day
Apr 2- Good Friday
Apr 5 - Easter Monday
April 25 - Anzac Day
Jun 7 - Queen's Birthday
Oct 25 - Labour Day

**UNITED KINGDOM**
May 1 - Labour Day
May 3 - May Day
May 31 - Spring Bank Holiday
Jun 13 Queens Birthday
Aug 30 - Bank Holiday
Nov 3 - St Andrew's Day
Dec 28 - Boxing Day Holiday

**USA**
Jan 18 - Martin Luther King Jr. Day
Feb 195- Presidents' Day
Apr 16 - Emancipation Day
May 31 - Memorial Day
Jul 4 - Independence Day Holiday
Oct 11 - Columbus Day
Nov 11 - Veterans Day
Nov 25 - Thanks Giving Day

**FRANCE & GERMANY**
May 8 - Victory Day
May 13 - Ascension Day
May 23~24 - Whit Sunday & Mon
Jul 14 - Bastille Day
Nov 1 - All Saints' Day
Nov 11 - Armistice Day

**GERMANY**
Aug 15 - Assumption Day
Jun 3 - Corpus Christi
Oct 3 - German Unity
Oct 31 - Reformation Day

# PUBLIC HOLIDAYS 2021

## ASIAN OBSERVATIONS
Feb 12 -15 - Chinese Lunar New Year
May 26 - Buddha's Birthday

## HONG KONG/CHINA
Jul 1 - HKSAR  (Establishment Day)
Feb - Lattern Festival (15th Day of Month 1 - Lunar calendar)
Apr 4 - Qing Ming Jie(Tomb Sweeping Festival)
Apr 10 - Good Friday
Apr 11 - Easter Saturday
Apr 13 - Easter Monday
May 1 - Labour Day
June 14 - (Tuen Ng) Dragon Boat Festival
Sept 21 - Mid-Autumn Festival
Oct 1 - National Day
Oct 14 - Chung Yeung Festival & holiday

## KOREA
Feb 12~14 - SolNal (Korean New Year)
Mar 1 - March 1st Movement Day
May 19 - Buddha's Birthday
May 5 - Children's Day
Jun 6 - Memorial Day
Aug 15 - Liberation Day
Sept 20~22 - Chusok (Korean Thanks Giving)
Oct 3 - National Foundation Day
Oct 9 - Hangeul Day
Dec 25 - Christmas Day

# LLWF BUCKET LIST

- [ ] 
- [ ] 
- [ ] 
- [ ] 
- [ ] 
- [ ] 
- [ ] 
- [ ] 
- [ ] 
- [ ] 
- [ ] 
- [ ] 
- [ ] 
- [ ] 
- [ ] 
- [ ] 
- [ ] 
- [ ] 
- [ ]

# LLWF NOTES

- [ ]
- [ ]
- [ ]
- [ ]
- [ ]
- [ ]
- [ ]
- [ ]
- [ ]
- [ ]
- [ ]
- [ ]
- [ ]
- [ ]
- [ ]
- [ ]
- [ ]
- [ ]
- [ ]

# LLWF TO DO LIST

- [ ] _____
- [ ] _____
- [ ] _____
- [ ] _____
- [ ] _____
- [ ] _____
- [ ] _____
- [ ] _____
- [ ] _____
- [ ] _____
- [ ] _____
- [ ] _____
- [ ] _____
- [ ] _____
- [ ] _____
- [ ] _____
- [ ] _____
- [ ] _____
- [ ] _____

# LLWF TO DO LIST

- [ ]
- [ ]
- [ ]
- [ ]
- [ ]
- [ ]
- [ ]
- [ ]
- [ ]
- [ ]
- [ ]
- [ ]
- [ ]
- [ ]
- [ ]
- [ ]
- [ ]
- [ ]

Monday | 월요일 | Lundi | 星期一 | Montag — 28

> IF YOU HAVE IMPROVED,
> JUST ONE PERSON'S
> LIFE,
> YOU HAVE MADE A
> DIFFERENCE.
> ...SKETA

#MakeItMonday

Tuesday | 화요일 | Mardi | 星期二 | Dienstag — 29

#TeamTuesday

Wednesday | 수요일 | Mercredi | 星期三 | Mittwoch — 30

#WCW

**31** Thursday | 목요일 | Jeidi | 星期四 | Donnerstag

#ThursdayThanks

**1** Friday | 금요일 | Vendredi | 星期五 | Freitag

#FamFriday

Saturday | 토요일
Samedi | 星期六 | Samstag **2**

#SaturdaySun

**3** Sunday | 일요일
Dimanche | 星期日 | Sonntag

#SoulSunday

# JANUARY

Monday | 월요일 | Lundi | 星期一 | Montag  4

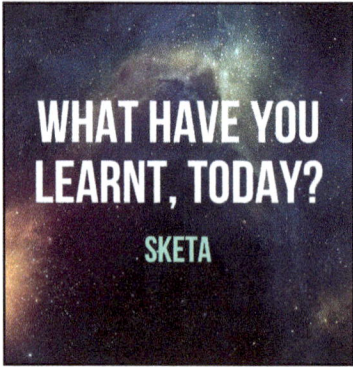

#MustDoMonday

Tuesday | 화요일 | Mardi | 星期二 | Dienstag  5

#TimeTravelTuesday

Wednesday | 수요일 | Mercredi | 星期三 | Mittwoch  6

#WednesdayWishes

**7**
Thursday | 목요일 | Jeidi | 星期四 | Donnerstag
#ThinkThursday

**8**
Friday | 금요일 | Vendredi | 星期五 | Freitag
#FameFriday

Saturday | 토요일
Samedi | 星期六 | Samstag  **9**
#SaveSaturday

**10** Sunday | 일요일
Dimanche | 星期日 | Sonntag
#SelinaSunday

# JANUARY

Monday | 월요일 | Lundi | 星期一 | Montag 〔11〕

#MakeItMonday

> *Build your dreams a*
> *reality to live in.*
>
> sketa

Tuesday | 화요일 | Mardi | 星期二 | Dienstag 〔12〕

#TeamTuesday

Wednesday | 수요일 | Mercredi | 星期三 | Mittwoch 〔13〕

#WCW

14 | Thursday | 목요일 | Jeidi | 星期四 | Donnerstag

#ThursdayThanks

15 | Friday | 금요일 | Vendredi | 星期五 | Freitag

#FamFriday

Saturday | 토요일
Samedi | 星期六 | Samstag | 16

17 | Dimanche | 星期日 | Sonntag
Sunday | 일요일

#SaturdaySun

#SoulSunday

Monday | 월요일 | Lundi | 星期一 | Montag | 18 |

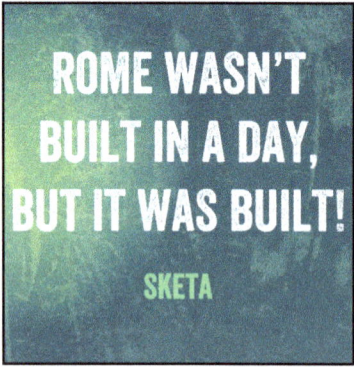

#MoveMonday

Tuesday | 화요일 | Mardi | 星期二 | Dienstag | 19 |

#TTTuesday

Wednesday | 수요일 | Mercredi | 星期三 | Mittwoch | 20 |

#WriteWednesday

**21** Thursday | 목요일 | Jeidi | 星期四 | Donnerstag

#ThoughtfulThursday

---

**22** Friday | 금요일 | Vendredi | 星期五 | Freitag

#FlyFriday

---

Saturday | 토요일
Samedi | 星期六 | Samstag  **23**  **24** Sunday | 일요일
Dimanche | 星期日 | Sonntag

#SuperSaturday                #SavourSunday

*JANUARY*

Monday | 월요일 | Lundi | 星期一 | Montag　　　　25

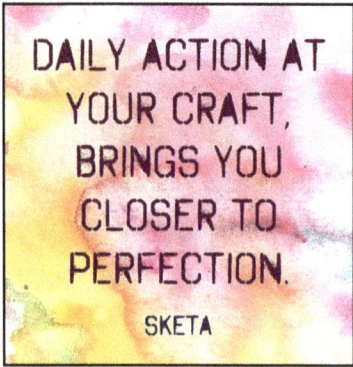

#MentorMonday

Tuesday | 화요일 | Mardi | 星期二 | Dienstag　　　26

#TeaTuesday

Wednesday | 수요일 | Mercredi | 星期三 | Mittwoch　　27

#Watercolour

**28**          Thursday | 목요일 | Jeidi | 星期四 | Donnerstag

#TeachThursday ──────────

**29**          Friday | 금요일 | Vendredi | 星期五 | Freitag

#FunFriday ──────────

Saturday | 토요일        **30**    **31**         Sunday | 일요일
Samedi | 星期六 | Samstag       Dimanche | 星期日 | Sonntag

#SketchSaturday ────────     #SillySunday ──────────

Monday | 월요일 | Lundi | 星期一 | Montag | 1 |

Life has a plan for you.
Even if you don't think it does.
Believe
Trust
Work hard
–
But don't blindly follow others.

Sketa

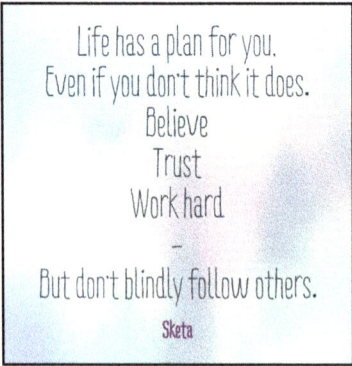

#MotivateMonday

Tuesday | 화요일 | Mardi | 星期二 | Dienstag | 2 |

#TheatreTuesday

Wednesday | 수요일 | Mercredi | 星期三 | Mittwoch | 3 |

#WorldWednesday

**4** Thursday | 목요일 | Jeidi | 星期四 | Donnerstag

#TravelThursday

**5** Friday | 금요일 | Vendredi | 星期五 | Freitag

#FilmFriday

Saturday | 토요일
Samedi | 星期六 | Samstag **6**

#SexySaturday

**7** Sunday | 일요일
Dimanche | 星期日 | Sonntag

#SleepSunday

Monday | 월요일 | Lundi | 星期一 | Montag

8

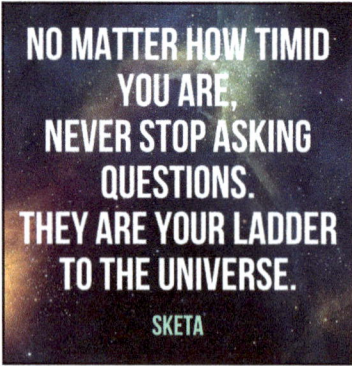

#MeMonday

Tuesday | 화요일 | Mardi | 星期二 | Dienstag

9

#TrumpTuesday

Wednesday | 수요일 | Mercredi | 星期三 | Mittwoch

10

#WatchMeWednesday

**11** Thursday | 목요일 | Jeidi | 星期四 | Donnerstag

#TogetherThursday

**12** Friday | 금요일 | Vendredi | 星期五 | Freitag

#FrameFriday

Saturday | 토요일
Samedi | 星期六 | Samstag **13**

#ShopSaturday

**14** Sunday | 일요일
Dimanche | 星期日 | Sonntag

#SpiritSunday

FEBRUARY

Monday | 월요일 | Lundi | 星期一 | Montag    15

> Don't open the mouth of judgement, before you have walked a mile, in the shoes of others.
>
> Sketa

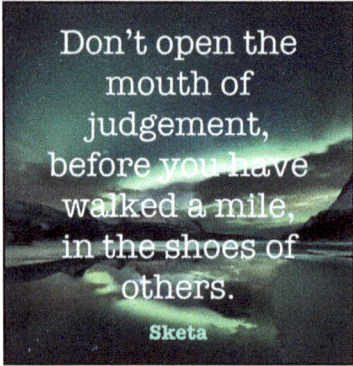

#MysteryMonday

Tuesday | 화요일 | Mardi | 星期二 | Dienstag    16

#TellAllTuesday

Wednesday | 수요일 | Mercredi | 星期三 | Mittwoch    17

#WiggleWednesday

**18** Thursday | 목요일 | Jeidi | 星期四 | Donnerstag

#ToDoThursday

**19** Friday | 금요일 | Vendredi | 星期五 | Freitag

#FatherFriday

Saturday | 토요일
Samedi | 星期六 | Samstag **20**

**21** Sunday | 일요일
Dimanche | 星期日 | Sonntag

#SportSaturday

#SongSunday

FEBRUARY

Monday | 월요일 | Lundi | 星期一 | Montag | 22

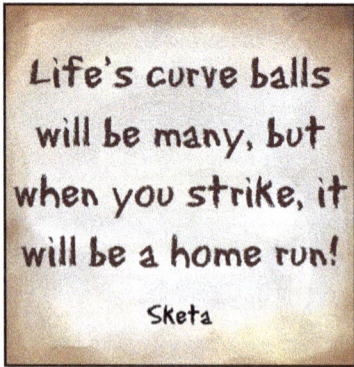

#MotherMonday

> Life's curve balls
> will be many, but
> when you strike, it
> will be a home run!
>
> Sketa

Tuesday | 화요일 | Mardi | 星期二 | Dienstag | 23

#TryTuesday

Wednesday | 수요일 | Mercredi | 星期三 | Mittwoch | 24

#WarriorWednesday

25 Thursday | 목요일 | Jeidi | 星期四 | Donnerstag

#ThrowbackThursday

26 Friday | 금요일 | Vendredi | 星期五 | Freitag

#FriendsFriday

Saturday | 토요일
Samedi | 星期六 | Samstag 27

28 Sunday | 일요일
Dimanche | 星期日 | Sonntag

#ShoutoutSaturday

#SacrificeSunday

MARCH

Monday | 월요일 | Lundi | 星期一 | Montag | 1 |

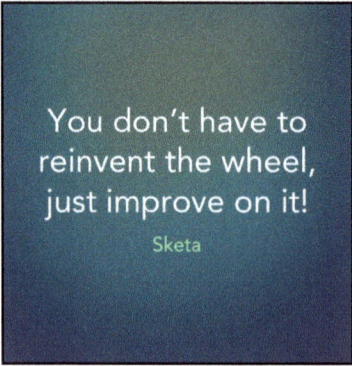

#MustDoMonday

You don't have to reinvent the wheel, just improve on it!
Sketa

Tuesday | 화요일 | Mardi | 星期二 | Dienstag | 2 |

#TimeTravelTuesday

Wednesday | 수요일 | Mercredi | 星期三 | Mittwoch | 3 |

#WednesdayWishes

**4** Thursday | 목요일 | Jeidi | 星期四 | Donnerstag

#ThinkThursday

**5** Friday | 금요일 | Vendredi | 星期五 | Freitag

#FameFriday

Saturday | 토요일
Samedi | 星期六 | Samstag **6**

#SaveSaturday

**7** Sunday | 일요일
Dimanche | 星期日 | Sonntag

#SelinaSunday

# MARCH

## Monday | 월요일 | Lundi | 星期一 | Montag — 8

> IF YOU HAVE IMPROVED, JUST ONE PERSON'S LIFE, YOU HAVE MADE A DIFFERENCE.
> ...SKETA

#MakeItMonday

## Tuesday | 화요일 | Mardi | 星期二 | Dienstag — 9

#TeamTuesday

## Wednesday | 수요일 | Mercredi | 星期三 | Mittwoch — 10

#WCW

**11**
Thursday | 목요일 | Jeidi | 星期四 | Donnerstag
#ThursdayThanks

**12**
Friday | 금요일 | Vendredi | 星期五 | Freitag
#FamFriday

Saturday | 토요일
Samedi | 星期六 | Samstag  **13**
#SaturdaySun

**14** Sunday | 일요일
Dimanche | 星期日 | Sonntag
#SoulSunday

Monday | 월요일 | Lundi | 星期一 | Montag      15

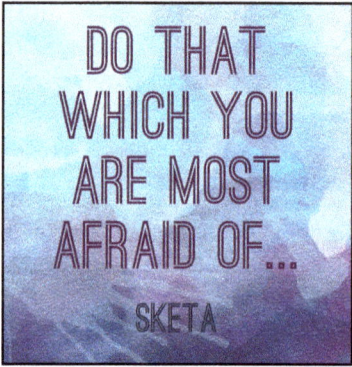

#MoveMonday

Tuesday | 화요일 | Mardi | 星期二 | Dienstag      16

#TTTuesday

Wednesday | 수요일 | Mercredi | 星期三 | Mittwoch      17

#WriteWednesday

18 Thursday | 목요일 | Jeidi | 星期四 | Donnerstag

#ThoughtfulThursday

19 Friday | 금요일 | Vendredi | 星期五 | Freitag

#FlyFriday

Saturday | 토요일
Samedi | 星期六 | Samstag　20

21 Sunday | 일요일
Dimanche | 星期日 | Sonntag

#SuperSaturday

#SavourSunday

Monday | 월요일 | Lundi | 星期一 | Montag      22

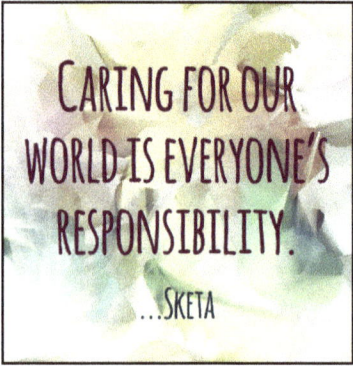

#MentorMonday

> CARING FOR OUR WORLD IS EVERYONE'S RESPONSIBILITY.
> ...SKETA

Tuesday | 화요일 | Mardi | 星期二 | Dienstag      23

#TeaTuesday

Wednesday | 수요일 | Mercredi | 星期三 | Mittwoch      24

#Watercolour

**25**
Thursday | 목요일 | Jeidi | 星期四 | Donnerstag
#TeachThursday

**26**
Friday | 금요일 | Vendredi | 星期五 | Freitag
#FunFriday

Saturday | 토요일
Samedi | 星期六 | Samstag **27**

**28** Sunday | 일요일
Dimanche | 星期日 | Sonntag
#SketchSaturday

#SillySunday

Monday | 월요일 | Lundi | 星期一 | Montag

29

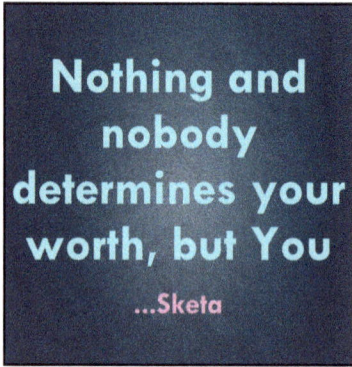

#MotivateMonday

> Nothing and nobody determines your worth, but You
> ...Sketa

Tuesday | 화요일 | Mardi | 星期二 | Dienstag

30

#TheatreTuesday

Wednesday | 수요일 | Mercredi | 星期三 | Mittwoch

31

#WorldWednesday

**1** Thursday | 목요일 | Jeidi | 星期四 | Donnerstag

#TravelThursday

**2** Friday | 금요일 | Vendredi | 星期五 | Freitag

#FilmFriday

Saturday | 토요일
Samedi | 星期六 | Samstag **3**

#SexySaturday

**4** Sunday | 일요일
Dimanche | 星期日 | Sonntag

#SleepSunday

APRIL

Monday | 월요일 | Lundi | 星期一 | Montag

5

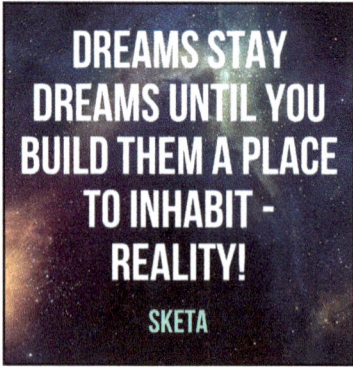

#MeMonday

Tuesday | 화요일 | Mardi | 星期二 | Dienstag

6

#TrumpTuesday

Wednesday | 수요일 | Mercredi | 星期三 | Mittwoch

7

#WatchMeWednesday

**8** Thursday | 목요일 | Jeidi | 星期四 | Donnerstag

#TogetherThursday ———————

**9** Friday | 금요일 | Vendredi | 星期五 | Freitag

#FrameFriday ———

Saturday | 토요일
Samedi | 星期六 | Samstag **10**

**11** Sunday | 일요일
Dimanche | 星期日 | Sonntag

#ShopSaturday ———————

#SpiritSunday ———————

## Monday | 월요일 | Lundi | 星期一 | Montag                    12

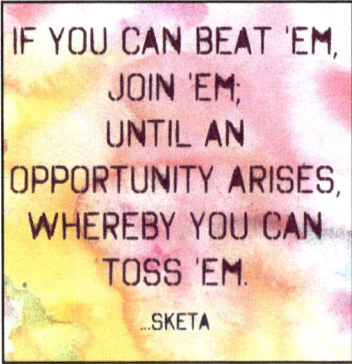

IF YOU CAN BEAT 'EM,
JOIN 'EM;
UNTIL AN
OPPORTUNITY ARISES,
WHEREBY YOU CAN
TOSS 'EM.
...SKETA

#MysteryMonday

## Tuesday | 화요일 | Mardi | 星期二 | Dienstag                    13

#TellAllTuesday

## Wednesday | 수요일 | Mercredi | 星期三 | Mittwoch                    14

#WiggleWednesday

**15** Thursday | 목요일 | Jeidi | 星期四 | Donnerstag

#ToDoThursday

**16** Friday | 금요일 | Vendredi | 星期五 | Freitag

#FatherFriday

Saturday | 토요일
Samedi | 星期六 | Samstag **17**

**18** Sunday | 일요일
Dimanche | 星期日 | Sonntag

#SportSaturday

#SongSunday

# APRIL

Monday | 월요일 | Lundi | 星期一 | Montag  **19**

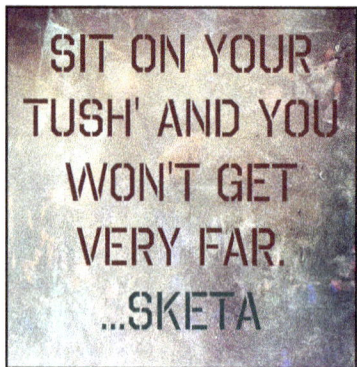

#MotherMonday

> SIT ON YOUR TUSH' AND YOU WON'T GET VERY FAR.
> ...SKETA

Tuesday | 화요일 | Mardi | 星期二 | Dienstag  **20**

#TryTuesday

Wednesday | 수요일 | Mercredi | 星期三 | Mittwoch  **21**

#WarriorWednesday

**22** Thursday | 목요일 | Jeidi | 星期四 | Donnerstag

#ThrowbackThursday

**23** Friday | 금요일 | Vendredi | 星期五 | Freitag

#FriendsFriday

Saturday | 토요일
Samedi | 星期六 | Samstag **24**

#ShoutoutSaturday

**25** Sunday | 일요일
Dimanche | 星期日 | Sonntag

#SacrificeSunday

APRIL

Monday | 월요일 | Lundi | 星期一 | Montag    26

WHO YOU BECOME IS ABOUT WHAT YOU DO TODAY; NOT WHAT YOU DO TOMORROW!

...SKETA

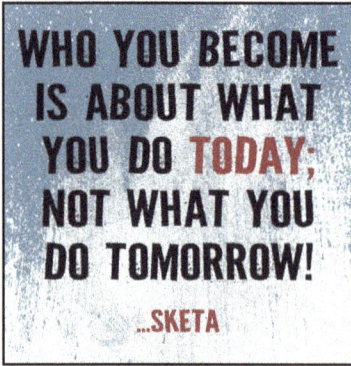

#MustDoMonday

Tuesday | 화요일 | Mardi | 星期二 | Dienstag    27

#TimeTravelTuesday

Wednesday | 수요일 | Mercredi | 星期三 | Mittwoch    28

#WednesdayWishes

**29** Thursday | 목요일 | Jeidi | 星期四 | Donnerstag

#ThinkThursday

**30** Friday | 금요일 | Vendredi | 星期五 | Freitag

#FameFriday

Saturday | 토요일
Samedi | 星期六 | Samstag **1**

**2** Sunday | 일요일
Dimanche | 星期日 | Sonntag

#SaveSaturday

#SelinaSunday

Monday | 월요일 | Lundi | 星期一 | Montag | 3

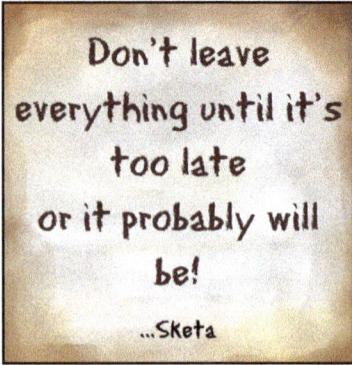

> Don't leave everything until it's too late or it probably will be!
> ...Sketa

#MakeItMonday

Tuesday | 화요일 | Mardi | 星期二 | Dienstag | 4

#TeamTuesday

Wednesday | 수요일 | Mercredi | 星期三 | Mittwoch | 5

#WCW

**6**
Thursday | 목요일 | Jeidi | 星期四 | Donnerstag

#ThursdayThanks

**7**
Friday | 금요일 | Vendredi | 星期五 | Freitag

#FamFriday

Saturday | 토요일
Samedi | 星期六 | Samstag  **8**

#SaturdaySun

**9** Sunday | 일요일
Dimanche | 星期日 | Sonntag

#SoulSunday

Monday | 월요일 | Lundi | 星期一 | Montag  **10**

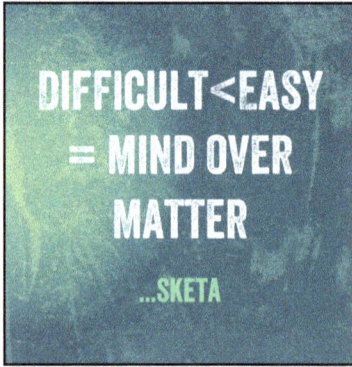

#MoveMonday

Tuesday | 화요일 | Mardi | 星期二 | Dienstag  **11**

#TTTuesday

Wednesday | 수요일 | Mercredi | 星期三 | Mittwoch  **12**

#WriteWednesday

**13** Thursday | 목요일 | Jeidi | 星期四 | Donnerstag

#ThoughtfulThursday

**14** Friday | 금요일 | Vendredi | 星期五 | Freitag

#FlyFriday

Saturday | 토요일
Samedi | 星期六 | Samstag **15**

#SuperSaturday

**16** Sunday | 일요일
Dimanche | 星期日 | Sonntag

#SavourSunday

MAY

Monday | 월요일 | Lundi | 星期一 | Montag          17

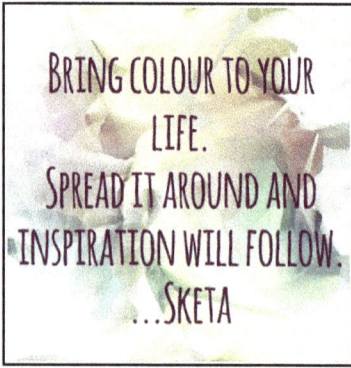

#MentorMonday

BRING COLOUR TO YOUR
LIFE.
SPREAD IT AROUND AND
INSPIRATION WILL FOLLOW.
...SKETA

Tuesday | 화요일 | Mardi | 星期二 | Dienstag          18

#TeaTuesday

Wednesday | 수요일 | Mercredi | 星期三 | Mittwoch

                                                  19

#Watercolour

**20** Thursday | 목요일 | Jeidi | 星期四 | Donnerstag
#TeachThursday

**21** Friday | 금요일 | Vendredi | 星期五 | Freitag
#FunFriday

Saturday | 토요일
Samedi | 星期六 | Samstag **22**
#SketchSaturday

Sunday | 일요일
**23** Dimanche | 星期日 | Sonntag
#SillySunday

MAY

Monday | 월요일 | Lundi | 星期一 | Montag | 24

#MotivateMonday

Life is made up of precious **moments.**
Each remembered, shared with and contributed to the lives of others.
Let each moment, **reflect** the best possible version of **'you'.**

...Sketa

Tuesday | 화요일 | Mardi | 星期二 | Dienstag | 25

#TheatreTuesday

Wednesday | 수요일 | Mercredi | 星期三 | Mittwoch | 26

#WorldWednesday

**27** Thursday | 목요일 | Jeidi | 星期四 | Donnerstag

#TravelThursday

**28** Friday | 금요일 | Vendredi | 星期五 | Freitag

#FilmFriday

Saturday | 토요일
Samedi | 星期六 | Samstag **29**

#SexySaturday

**30** Sunday | 일요일
Dimanche | 星期日 | Sonntag

#SleepSunday

Monday | 월요일 | Lundi | 星期一 | Montag

31

#MeMonday

Tuesday | 화요일 | Mardi | 星期二 | Dienstag

1

#TrumpTuesday

Wednesday | 수요일 | Mercredi | 星期三 | Mittwoch

2

#WatchMeWednesday

**3** Thursday | 목요일 | Jeidi | 星期四 | Donnerstag

#TogetherThursday

**4** Friday | 금요일 | Vendredi | 星期五 | Freitag

#FrameFriday

Saturday | 토요일
Samedi | 星期六 | Samstag  **5**

#ShopSaturday

**6** Sunday | 일요일
Dimanche | 星期日 | Sonntag

#SpiritSunday

Monday | 월요일 | Lundi | 星期一 | Montag          7

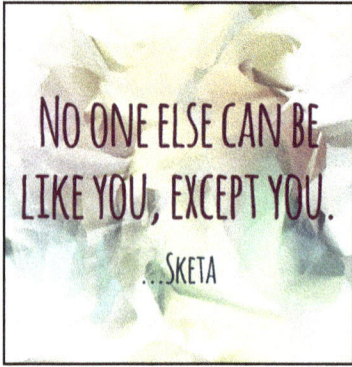

#MysteryMonday

> NO ONE ELSE CAN BE LIKE YOU, EXCEPT YOU.
> ...SKETA

Tuesday | 화요일 | Mardi | 星期二 | Dienstag          8

#TellAllTuesday

Wednesday | 수요일 | Mercredi | 星期三 | Mittwoch          9

#WiggleWednesday

**10** Thursday | 목요일 | Jeidi | 星期四 | Donnerstag

#ToDoThursday

**11** Friday | 금요일 | Vendredi | 星期五 | Freitag

#FatherFriday

Saturday | 토요일
Samedi | 星期六 | Samstag **12**

**13** Sunday | 일요일
Dimanche | 星期日 | Sonntag

#SportSaturday

#SongSunday

Monday | 월요일 | Lundi | 星期一 | Montag                          14

**MAKING SENSE OF THE
WORLD AND ITS
INHABITANTS
TAKES GRIT, RESILIENCE
AND PATIENCE,
BUT MOST OF ALL KINDNESS.**

...SKETA

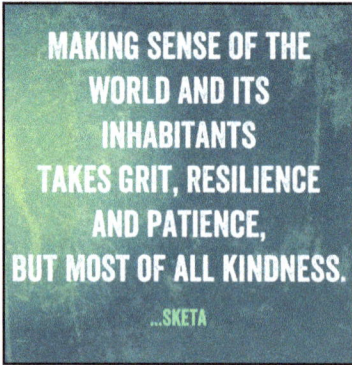

#MotherMonday

Tuesday | 화요일 | Mardi | 星期二 | Dienstag                    15

#TryTuesday

Wednesday | 수요일 | Mercredi | 星期三 | Mittwoch              16

#WarriorWednesday

**17** Thursday | 목요일 | Jeidi | 星期四 | Donnerstag

#ThrowbackThursday

**18** Friday | 금요일 | Vendredi | 星期五 | Freitag

#FriendsFriday

Saturday | 토요일
Samedi | 星期六 | Samstag **17**

**20** Sunday | 일요일
Dimanche | 星期日 | Sonntag

#ShoutoutSaturday

#SacrificeSunday

## Monday | 월요일 | Lundi | 星期一 | Montag

21

You need to break a bad habit?
Never engage in negative people; surround yourself
with only positive; find an alternative to the bad
habit you want to break; sleep well and regulate your
sleep patterns to your bio-rhythms; get adequate
exercise and engage with the human race; workout
what promotes your bad habit and avoid it at all
costs; find a something or someone to keep you
accountable; believe that in all situations you have
something to learn; believe in yourself, your abilities,
your intelligence and your maker that your can
accomplish great things (you can always do and be
more than you think you can) and above all – nothing
happens without you taking the first step – the
rest is just maintenance!
Skets

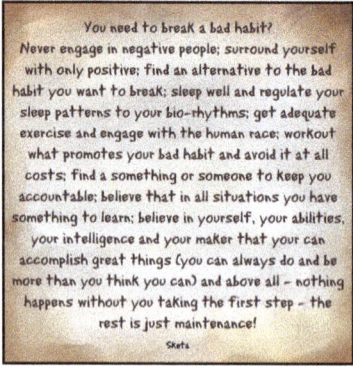

#MustDoMonday

## Tuesday | 화요일 | Mardi | 星期二 | Dienstag

22

#TimeTravelTuesday

## Wednesday | 수요일 | Mercredi | 星期三 | Mittwoch

23

#WednesdayWishes

**24**

Thursday | 목요일 | Jeidi | 星期四 | Donnerstag

#ThinkThursday

**25**

Friday | 금요일 | Vendredi | 星期五 | Freitag

#FameFriday

Saturday | 토요일
Samedi | 星期六 | Samstag  **26**

**27** Sunday | 일요일
Dimanche | 星期日 | Sonntag

#SaveSaturday

#SelinaSunday

Monday | 월요일 | Lundi | 星期一 | Montag ___ 28

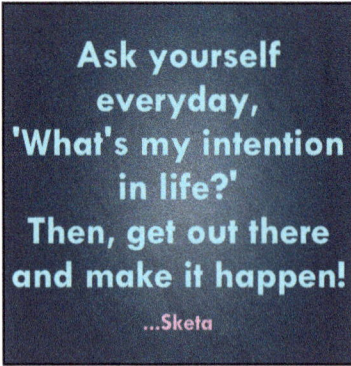

Ask yourself everyday, 'What's my intention in life?' Then, get out there and make it happen! ...Sketa

#MakeItMonday

Tuesday | 화요일 | Mardi | 星期二 | Dienstag ___ 29

#TeamTuesday

Wednesday | 수요일 | Mercredi | 星期三 | Mittwoch ___ 30

#WCW

**1** Thursday | 목요일 | Jeidi | 星期四 | Donnerstag

#ThursdayThanks

---

**2** Friday | 금요일 | Vendredi | 星期五 | Freitag

#FamFriday

---

Saturday | 토요일
Samedi | 星期六 | Samstag  **3**   **4** Dimanche | 星期日 | Sonntag

Sunday | 일요일

#SaturdaySun

#SoulSunday

Monday | 월요일 | Lundi | 星期一 | Montag | 5 |

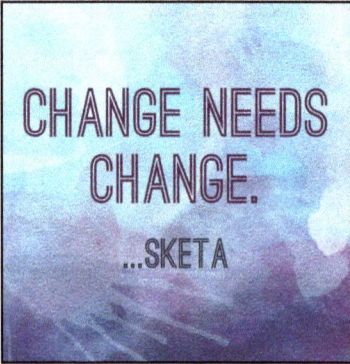

#MoveMonday

Tuesday | 화요일 | Mardi | 星期二 | Dienstag | 6 |

#TTTuesday

Wednesday | 수요일 | Mercredi | 星期三 | Mittwoch | 7 |

#WriteWednesday

**8** Thursday | 목요일 | Jeidi | 星期四 | Donnerstag

#ThoughtfulThursday

**9** Friday | 금요일 | Vendredi | 星期五 | Freitag

#FlyFriday

Saturday | 토요일
Samedi | 星期六 | Samstag **10**

#SuperSaturday

Sunday | 일요일
**11** Dimanche | 星期日 | Sonntag

#SavourSunday

Monday | 월요일 | Lundi | 星期一 | Montag    `12`

*Build your dreams a reality to live in.*

sketa

#MentorMonday

Tuesday | 화요일 | Mardi | 星期二 | Dienstag    `13`

#TeaTuesday

Wednesday | 수요일 | Mercredi | 星期三 | Mittwoch    `14`

#Watercolour

**15** Thursday | 목요일 | Jeidi | 星期四 | Donnerstag

#TeachThursday

**16** Friday | 금요일 | Vendredi | 星期五 | Freitag

#FunFriday

Saturday | 토요일
Samedi | 星期六 | Samstag **17**

#SketchSaturday

**18** Sunday | 일요일
Dimanche | 星期日 | Sonntag

#SillySunday

Monday | 월요일 | Lundi | 星期一 | Montag  `19`

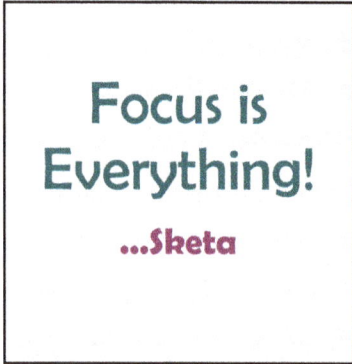

#MotivateMonday

**Focus is Everything!**
**...Sketa**

Tuesday | 화요일 | Mardi | 星期二 | Dienstag  `20`

#TheatreTuesday

Wednesday | 수요일 | Mercredi | 星期三 | Mittwoch  `21`

#WorldWednesday

**22** Thursday | 목요일 | Jeidi | 星期四 | Donnerstag

#TravelThursday

**23** Friday | 금요일 | Vendredi | 星期五 | Freitag

#FilmFriday

Saturday | 토요일
Samedi | 星期六 | Samstag **24**

**25** Sunday | 일요일
Dimanche | 星期日 | Sonntag

#SexySaturday

#SleepSunday

## Monday | 월요일 | Lundi | 星期一 | Montag          26

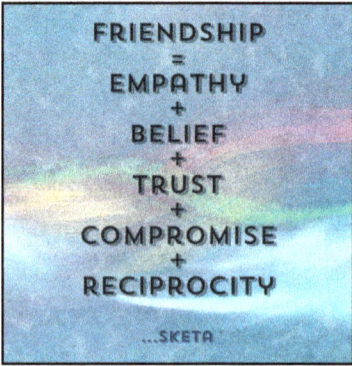

#MeMonday

## Tuesday | 화요일 | Mardi | 星期二 | Dienstag          27

#TrumpTuesday

## Wednesday | 수요일 | Mercredi | 星期三 | Mittwoch          28

#WatchMeWednesday

**29** Thursday | 목요일 | Jeidi | 星期四 | Donnerstag

#TogetherThursday

**30** Friday | 금요일 | Vendredi | 星期五 | Freitag

#FrameFriday

Saturday | 토요일
Samedi | 星期六 | Samstag  **31**

#ShopSaturday

**1** Sunday | 일요일
Dimanche | 星期日 | Sonntag

#SpiritSunday

Monday | 월요일 | Lundi | 星期一 | Montag ___ 2

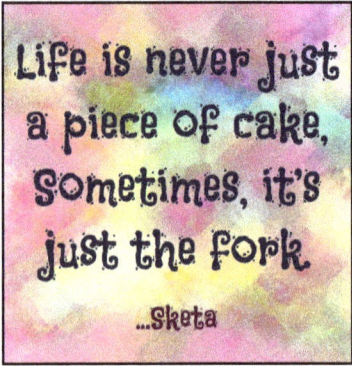

#MysteryMonday

> Life is never just
> a piece of cake,
> sometimes, it's
> just the fork
> ...Sketa

Tuesday | 화요일 | Mardi | 星期二 | Dienstag ___ 3

#TellAllTuesday

Wednesday | 수요일 | Mercredi | 星期三 | Mittwoch ___ 4

#WiggleWednesday

**5** Thursday | 목요일 | Jeidi | 星期四 | Donnerstag

#ToDoThursday

**6** Friday | 금요일 | Vendredi | 星期五 | Freitag

#FatherFriday

Saturday | 토요일
Samedi | 星期六 | Samstag **7**

**8** Sunday | 일요일
Dimanche | 星期日 | Sonntag

#SportSaturday

#SongSunday

# AUGUST

**Monday | 월요일 | Lundi | 星期一 | Montag**　9

ONE CAN NOT BE TRULY
THANKFUL FOR ONES
BLESSINGS
UNTIL ONE HAS SEEN BOTH
SIDES OF THE COIN.
...SKETA

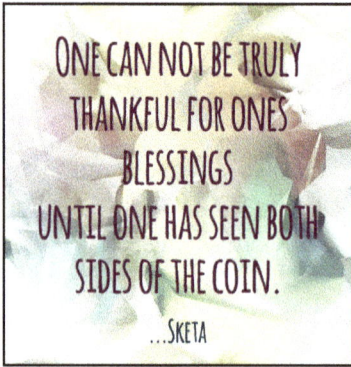

#MotherMonday

**Tuesday | 화요일 | Mardi | 星期二 | Dienstag**　10

#TryTuesday

**Wednesday | 수요일 | Mercredi | 星期三 | Mittwoch**　11

#WarriorWednesday

**12**       Thursday | 목요일 | Jeidi | 星期四 | Donnerstag

#ThrowbackThursday

**13**       Friday | 금요일 | Vendredi | 星期五 | Freitag

#FriendsFriday

Saturday | 토요일
Samedi | 星期六 | Samstag **14**

#ShoutoutSaturday

**15** Sunday | 일요일
Dimanche | 星期日 | Sonntag

#SacrificeSunday

Monday | 월요일 | Lundi | 星期一 | Montag  16

> We study life's tests everyday.
> The big ones will require all your attention, focus, resilience and energy you can muster.
> A Grade results aren't assured, but pass you must!
>
> Sketa

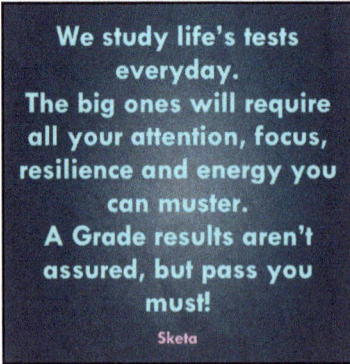

#MakeItMonday

Tuesday | 화요일 | Mardi | 星期二 | Dienstag  17

#TeamTuesday

Wednesday | 수요일 | Mercredi | 星期三 | Mittwoch  18

#WCW

**19** Thursday | 목요일 | Jeidi | 星期四 | Donnerstag
#ThursdayThanks

**20** Friday | 금요일 | Vendredi | 星期五 | Freitag
#FamFriday

Saturday | 토요일
Samedi | 星期六 | Samstag **21**
#SaturdaySun

**22** Sunday | 일요일
Dimanche | 星期日 | Sonntag
#SoulSunday

# AUGUST

Monday | 월요일 | Lundi | 星期一 | Montag    `23`

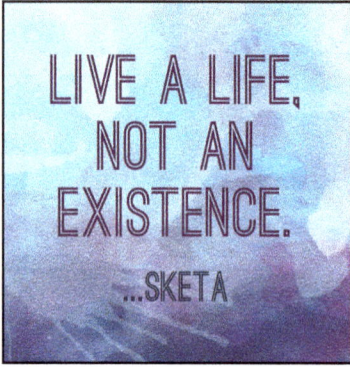

#MoveMonday

Tuesday | 화요일 | Mardi | 星期二 | Dienstag    `24`

#TTTuesday

Wednesday | 수요일 | Mercredi | 星期三 | Mittwoch    `25`

#WriteWednesday

**26** Thursday | 목요일 | Jeidi | 星期四 | Donnerstag

#ThoughtfulThursday

**27** Friday | 금요일 | Vendredi | 星期五 | Freitag

#FlyFriday

Saturday | 토요일
Samedi | 星期六 | Samstag **28**

#SuperSaturday

Sunday | 일요일
**29** Dimanche | 星期日 | Sonntag

#SavourSunday

# AUGUST

Monday | 월요일 | Lundi | 星期一 | Montag      30

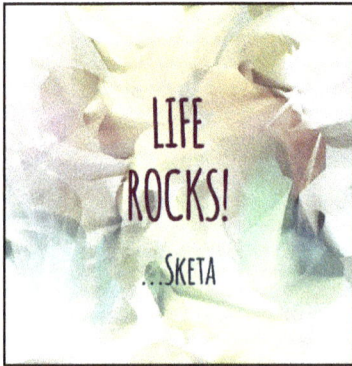

#MentorMonday

Tuesday | 화요일 | Mardi | 星期二 | Dienstag      31

#TeaTuesday

Wednesday | 수요일 | Mercredi | 星期三 | Mittwoch      1

#Watercolour

2 Thursday | 목요일 | Jeidi | 星期四 | Donnerstag

#TeachThursday

3 Friday | 금요일 | Vendredi | 星期五 | Freitag

#FunFriday

Saturday | 토요일
Samedi | 星期六 | Samstag  4

5 Sunday | 일요일
Dimanche | 星期日 | Sonntag

#SketchSaturday

#SillySunday

SEPTEMBER

Monday | 월요일 | Lundi | 星期一 | Montag

6

#MotivateMonday

Time is fleeting.
Make your life
miraculous!

...Sketa

Tuesday | 화요일 | Mardi | 星期二 | Dienstag

7

#TheatreTuesday

Wednesday | 수요일 | Mercredi | 星期三 | Mittwoch

8

#WorldWednesday

**9** Thursday | 목요일 | Jeidi | 星期四 | Donnerstag

#TravelThursday

**10** Friday | 금요일 | Vendredi | 星期五 | Freitag

#FilmFriday

Saturday | 토요일
Samedi | 星期六 | Samstag **11**

#SexySaturday

**12** Sunday | 일요일
Dimanche | 星期日 | Sonntag

#SleepSunday

SEPTEMBER

Monday | 월요일 | Lundi | 星期一 | Montag 　13

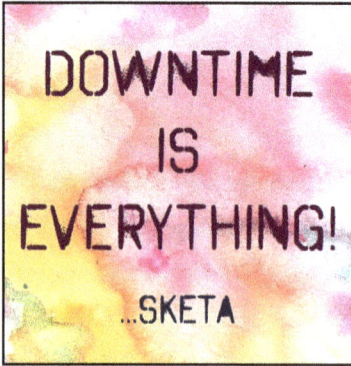

#MeMonday

Tuesday | 화요일 | Mardi | 星期二 | Dienstag 　14

#TrumpTuesday

Wednesday | 수요일 | Mercredi | 星期三 | Mittwoch 　15

#WatchMeWednesday

**16** Thursday | 목요일 | Jeidi | 星期四 | Donnerstag

#TogetherThursday

**17** Friday | 금요일 | Vendredi | 星期五 | Freitag

#FrameFriday

Saturday | 토요일
Samedi | 星期六 | Samstag **18**

Sunday | 일요일
**19** Dimanche | 星期日 | Sonntag

#ShopSaturday

#SpiritSunday

# SEPTEMBER

Monday | 월요일 | Lundi | 星期一 | Montag | 20

#MysteryMonday

> TO BE HUMBLE AND THANKFUL FOR ALL OUR BLESSINGS, IS THE GREATEST LESSON TO BE LEARNED.
> ...SKETA

Tuesday | 화요일 | Mardi | 星期二 | Dienstag | 21

#TellAllTuesday

Wednesday | 수요일 | Mercredi | 星期三 | Mittwoch | 22

#WiggleWednesday

23 Thursday | 목요일 | Jeidi | 星期四 | Donnerstag

#ToDoThursday

24 Friday | 금요일 | Vendredi | 星期五 | Freitag

#FatherFriday

Saturday | 토요일
Samedi | 星期六 | Samstag 25

#SportSaturday

Sunday | 일요일
26 Dimanche | 星期日 | Sonntag

#SongSunday

Monday | 월요일 | Lundi | 星期一 | Montag

27

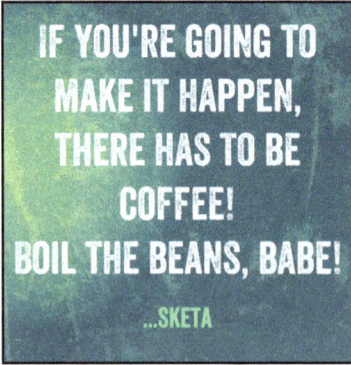

IF YOU'RE GOING TO
MAKE IT HAPPEN,
THERE HAS TO BE
COFFEE!
BOIL THE BEANS, BABE!
...SKETA

#MotherMonday

Tuesday | 화요일 | Mardi | 星期二 | Dienstag

28

#TryTuesday

Wednesday | 수요일 | Mercredi | 星期三 | Mittwoch

29

#WarriorWednesday

**30** Thursday | 목요일 | Jeidi | 星期四 | Donnerstag

#ThrowbackThursday

**1** Friday | 금요일 | Vendredi | 星期五 | Freitag

#FriendsFriday

Saturday | 토요일
Samedi | 星期六 | Samstag **2**

#ShoutoutSaturday

**3** Sunday | 일요일
Dimanche | 星期日 | Sonntag

#SacrificeSunday

## Monday | 월요일 | Lundi | 星期一 | Montag

4

> PRIORITIES ARE
> EVERYTHING YOU'RE
> DOING NOW. IF THAT'S
> NOT WHAT YOU WANT
> OR WHERE YOU WANT TO
> BE TEN YEARS FROM NOW
> –
> CHANGE YOUR LINE OF
> **THINKING!**
> ...SKETA

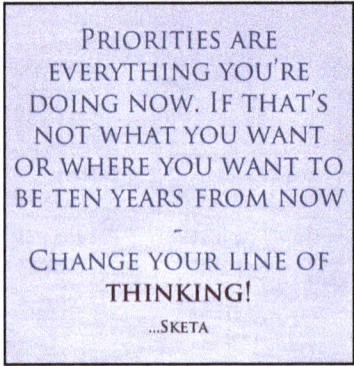

#MustDoMonday

## Tuesday | 화요일 | Mardi | 星期二 | Dienstag

5

#TimeTravelTuesday

## Wednesday | 수요일 | Mercredi | 星期三 | Mittwoch

6

#WednesdayWishes

**7**

Thursday | 목요일 | Jeidi | 星期四 | Donnerstag

#ThinkThursday

**8**

Friday | 금요일 | Vendredi | 星期五 | Freitag

#FameFriday

Saturday | 토요일
Samedi | 星期六 | Samstag   **9**

**10** Dimanche | 星期日 | Sonntag
Sunday | 일요일

#SaveSaturday

#SelinaSunday

Monday | 월요일 | Lundi | 星期一 | Montag 11

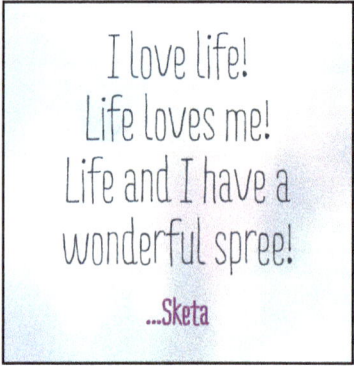

#MakeItMonday

Tuesday | 화요일 | Mardi | 星期二 | Dienstag 12

#TeamTuesday

Wednesday | 수요일 | Mercredi | 星期三 | Mittwoch 13

#WCW

**14** Thursday | 목요일 | Jeidi | 星期四 | Donnerstag

#ThursdayThanks

---

**15** Friday | 금요일 | Vendredi | 星期五 | Freitag

#FamFriday

---

Saturday | 토요일
Samedi | 星期六 | Samstag  **16**

**17** Sunday | 일요일
Dimanche | 星期日 | Sonntag

#SaturdaySun

#SoulSunday

Monday | 월요일 | Lundi | 星期一 | Montag

18

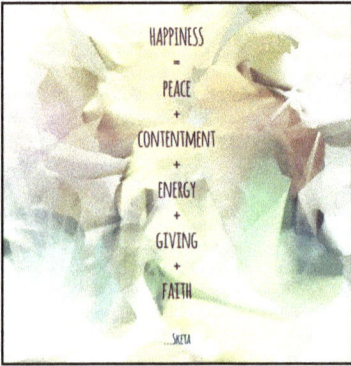

#MoveMonday

Tuesday | 화요일 | Mardi | 星期二 | Dienstag

19

#TTTuesday

Wednesday | 수요일 | Mercredi | 星期三 | Mittwoch

20

#WriteWednesday

**21**          Thursday | 목요일 | Jeidi | 星期四 | Donnerstag

#ThoughtfulThursday

**22**          Friday | 금요일 | Vendredi | 星期五 | Freitag

#FlyFriday

Saturday | 토요일
Samedi | 星期六 | Samstag   **23**    **24** Dimanche | 星期日 | Sonntag

Sunday | 일요일

#SuperSaturday            #SavourSunday

Monday | 월요일 | Lundi | 星期一 | Montag **25**

WE MIGHT NOT BE
WHERE WE WANT TO
BE,
BUT WE ARE WHERE
WE ARE MEANT TO BE
...TO GROW
...SKETA

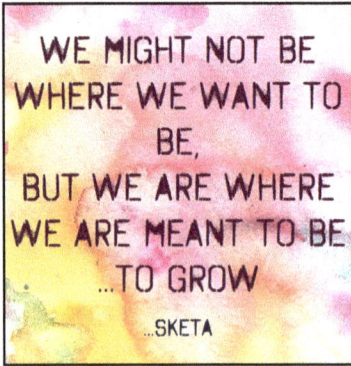

#MentorMonday

Tuesday | 화요일 | Mardi | 星期二 | Dienstag **26**

#TeaTuesday

Wednesday | 수요일 | Mercredi | 星期三 | Mittwoch **27**

#Watercolour

**28** Thursday | 목요일 | Jeidi | 星期四 | Donnerstag

#TeachThursday

**29** Friday | 금요일 | Vendredi | 星期五 | Freitag

#FunFriday

Saturday | 토요일
Samedi | 星期六 | Samstag **30**

#SketchSaturday

**31** Sunday | 일요일
Dimanche | 星期日 | Sonntag

#SillySunday

Monday | 월요일 | Lundi | 星期一 | Montag | 1 |

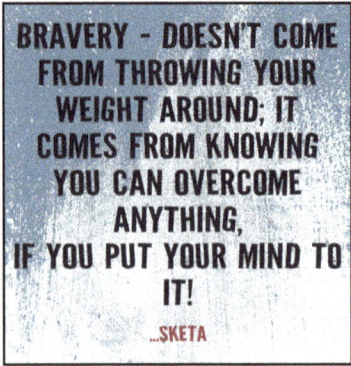

#MotivateMonday

BRAVERY - DOESN'T COME FROM THROWING YOUR WEIGHT AROUND; IT COMES FROM KNOWING YOU CAN OVERCOME ANYTHING, IF YOU PUT YOUR MIND TO IT!
...SKETA

Tuesday | 화요일 | Mardi | 星期二 | Dienstag | 2 |

#TheatreTuesday

Wednesday | 수요일 | Mercredi | 星期三 | Mittwoch | 3 |

#WorldWednesday

**4**

Thursday | 목요일 | Jeidi | 星期四 | Donnerstag

#TravelThursday

---

**5**

Friday | 금요일 | Vendredi | 星期五 | Freitag

#FilmFriday

---

Saturday | 토요일
Samedi | 星期六 | Samstag   **6**

#SexySaturday

**7** | Dimanche | 星期日 | Sonntag
Sunday | 일요일

#SleepSunday

NOVEMBER

Monday | 월요일 | Lundi | 星期一 | Montag — 8

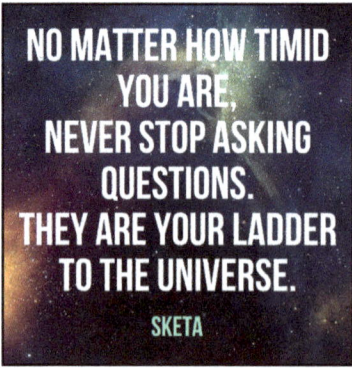

#MeMonday

Tuesday | 화요일 | Mardi | 星期二 | Dienstag — 9

#TrumpTuesday

Wednesday | 수요일 | Mercredi | 星期三 | Mittwoch — 10

#WatchMeWednesday

**11** Thursday | 목요일 | Jeidi | 星期四 | Donnerstag

#TogetherThursday

**12** Friday | 금요일 | Vendredi | 星期五 | Freitag

#FrameFriday

Saturday | 토요일
Samedi | 星期六 | Samstag **13**

#ShopSaturday

**14** Sunday | 일요일
Dimanche | 星期日 | Sonntag

#SpiritSunday

Monday | 월요일 | Lundi | 星期一 | Montag | 15 |

> There is no such thing as being lost. if you know where your feet stand. where your heart beats and your head lies. there is no lost – only direction to be sought to see where you grow best!
>
> ...Sketa

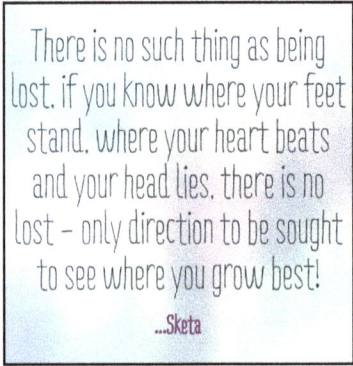

#MysteryMonday

Tuesday | 화요일 | Mardi | 星期二 | Dienstag | 16 |

#TellAllTuesday

Wednesday | 수요일 | Mercredi | 星期三 | Mittwoch | 17 |

#WiggleWednesday

**18** Thursday | 목요일 | Jeidi | 星期四 | Donnerstag

#ToDoThursday

**19** Friday | 금요일 | Vendredi | 星期五 | Freitag

#FatherFriday

Saturday | 토요일
Samedi | 星期六 | Samstag  **20**

#SportSaturday

**21** Sunday | 일요일
Dimanche | 星期日 | Sonntag

#SongSunday

NOVEMBER

Monday | 월요일 | Lundi | 星期一 | Montag — 22

Inequality is not borne
out of circumstance.
It is born out of narrow-
minded individuals;
Who thrive on bully
mentality,
Who can not see past
their own insecurities.
...Sketa

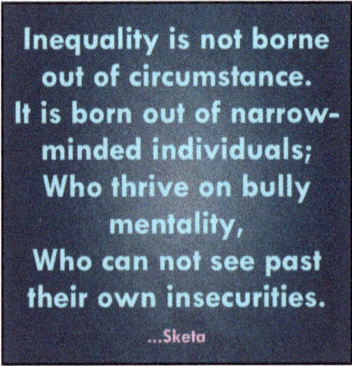

#MotherMonday

Tuesday | 화요일 | Mardi | 星期二 | Dienstag — 23

#TryTuesday

Wednesday | 수요일 | Mercredi | 星期三 | Mittwoch — 24

#WarriorWednesday

**25** Thursday | 목요일 | Jeidi | 星期四 | Donnerstag

#ThrowbackThursday

**26** Friday | 금요일 | Vendredi | 星期五 | Freitag

#FriendsFriday

Saturday | 토요일
Samedi | 星期六 | Samstag  **27**

#ShoutoutSaturday

**28** Sunday | 일요일
Dimanche | 星期日 | Sonntag

#SacrificeSunday

NOVEMBER

Monday | 월요일 | Lundi | 星期一 | Montag                              29

#MustDoMonday

> EVERYDAY, I GIVE THANKS
> FOR MY LIFE; MY HEALTH,
> FAMILY AND FRIENDS; MY
> JOURNEY AND CREATOR.
> SKETA

Tuesday | 화요일 | Mardi | 星期二 | Dienstag                         30

#TimeTravelTuesday

Wednesday | 수요일 | Mercredi | 星期三 | Mittwoch                     1

#WednesdayWishes

**2**

Thursday | 목요일 | Jeidi | 星期四 | Donnerstag

#ThinkThursday

**3**

Friday | 금요일 | Vendredi | 星期五 | Freitag

#FameFriday

Saturday | 토요일
Samedi | 星期六 | Samstag  **4**

**5**  Sunday | 일요일
Dimanche | 星期日 | Sonntag

#SaveSaturday

#SelinaSunday

## DECEMBER

Monday | 월요일 | Lundi | 星期一 | Montag   6

We are not bound by the here-say of others; nor by the abilities bound to our person, but by our lack of vision to see outside the realm of what is possible, probable or highly likely had we taken that step to believe in a dream.

*Sketa*

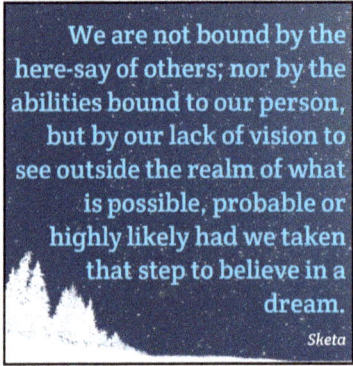

#MakeItMonday

Tuesday | 화요일 | Mardi | 星期二 | Dienstag   7

#TeamTuesday

Wednesday | 수요일 | Mercredi | 星期三 | Mittwoch   8

#WCW

**9** Thursday | 목요일 | Jeidi | 星期四 | Donnerstag

#ThursdayThanks

**10** Friday | 금요일 | Vendredi | 星期五 | Freitag

#FamFriday

Saturday | 토요일
Samedi | 星期六 | Samstag **11**

#SaturdaySun

**12** Sunday | 일요일
Dimanche | 星期日 | Sonntag

#SoulSunday

*DECEMBER*

Monday | 월요일 | Lundi | 星期一 | Montag 　13

GOALS...
TO BE BETTER THAN I WAS YESTERDAY; MORE FOCUSED THAN I WAS A MINUTE AGO; MORE RESILIENT THAN I WAS A YEAR AGO.
TO ACHIEVE MORE THAN I DID YESTERDAY; CREATE MORE THAN I DID A MINUTE AGO; SUCCEED WHERE I FAILED A YEAR AGO.

SKETA

#MoveMonday

Tuesday | 화요일 | Mardi | 星期二 | Dienstag 　14

#TTTuesday

Wednesday | 수요일 | Mercredi | 星期三 | Mittwoch 　15

#WriteWednesday

**16** Thursday | 목요일 | Jeidi | 星期四 | Donnerstag

#ThoughtfulThursday

**17** Friday | 금요일 | Vendredi | 星期五 | Freitag

#FlyFriday

Saturday | 토요일
Samedi | 星期六 | Samstag **18**

#SuperSaturday

Sunday | 일요일
**19** Dimanche | 星期日 | Sonntag

#SavourSunday

DECEMBER

Monday | 월요일 | Lundi | 星期一 | Montag | 20

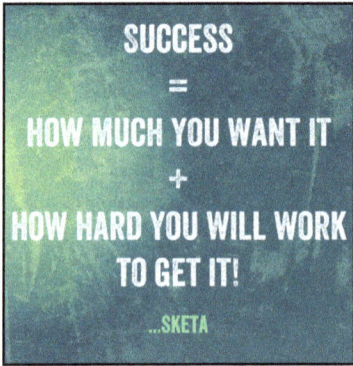

#MentorMonday

Tuesday | 화요일 | Mardi | 星期二 | Dienstag | 21

#TeaTuesday

Wednesday | 수요일 | Mercredi | 星期三 | Mittwoch | 22

#Watercolour

**23** Thursday | 목요일 | Jeidi | 星期四 | Donnerstag

#TeachThursday

---

**24** Friday | 금요일 | Vendredi | 星期五 | Freitag

#FunFriday

---

Saturday | 토요일
Samedi | 星期六 | Samstag **25**

#SketchSaturday

**26** Sunday | 일요일
Dimanche | 星期日 | Sonntag

#SillySunday

# DECEMBER

Monday | 월요일 | Lundi | 星期一 | Montag   27

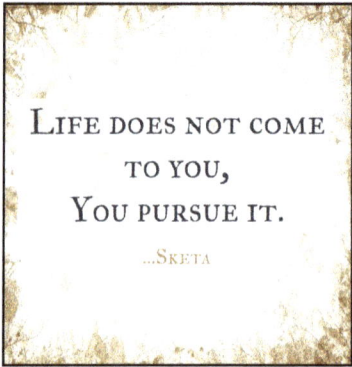

#MotivateMonday

LIFE DOES NOT COME
TO YOU,
YOU PURSUE IT.
...SKETA

Tuesday | 화요일 | Mardi | 星期二 | Dienstag   28

#TheatreTuesday

Wednesday | 수요일 | Mercredi | 星期三 | Mittwoch   29

#WorldWednesday

**30** Thursday | 목요일 | Jeidi | 星期四 | Donnerstag

#TravelThursday

**31** Friday | 금요일 | Vendredi | 星期五 | Freitag

#FilmFriday

Saturday | 토요일
Samedi | 星期六 | Samstag **1**

**2** Dimanche | 星期日 | Sonntag

Sunday | 일요일

#SexySaturday

#SleepSunday

Monday | 월요일 | Lundi | 星期一 | Montag

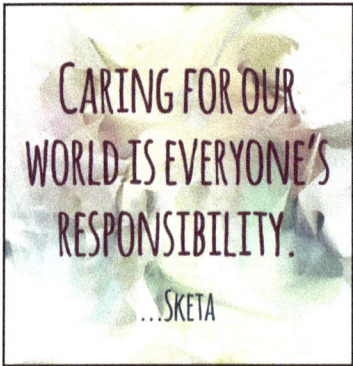

#MentorMonday

> CARING FOR OUR
> WORLD IS EVERYONE'S
> RESPONSIBILITY.
> ...SKETA

Tuesday | 화요일 | Mardi | 星期二 | Dienstag

4

#TeaTuesday

Wednesday | 수요일 | Mercredi | 星期三 | Mittwoch

5

#Watercolour

6 Thursday | 목요일 | Jeidi | 星期四 | Donnerstag

#TeachThursday

7 Friday | 금요일 | Vendredi | 星期五 | Freitag

#FunFriday

Saturday | 토요일
Samedi | 星期六 | Samstag  8

#SketchSaturday

9 Sunday | 일요일
Dimanche | 星期日 | Sonntag

#SillySunday

DO THAT
WHICH YOU
ARE MOST
AFRAID OF...

SKETA

DAILY ACTION AT
YOUR CRAFT,
BRINGS YOU
CLOSER TO
PERFECTION.

SKETA

Focus is
Everything!

CARI
WORLD
RESPC

LIFE
ROCKS!

...Sketa

ROME WASN'T
BUILT IN A DAY,
BUT IT WAS BUILT!

SKETA

Build y
reali

CHANGE NEEDS
CHANGE.

...SKETA

Focus is
Everything!

IF YOU CAN BEAT 'EM,
JOIN 'EM;
UNTIL AN
OPPORTUNITY ARISES,
WHEREBY YOU CAN
TOSS 'EM.

...SKETA

IF YOU H
JUST C

YOU H
DIF

R OUR
YONE'S
LITY.

DOWNTIME
IS
EVERYTHING!
...SKETA

Focus is
Everything!

CHANGE NEEDS
CHANGE.
...SKETA

reams a
ive in.

SUCCESS
=
HOW MUCH YOU WANT IT
+
HOW HARD YOU WILL WORK
TO GET IT!
...SKETA

LIFE
ROCKS!
...SKETA

IPROVED,
RSON'S

ADE A
CE.

Focus is
Everything!

EVERYDAY IS
A BLESSED
DAY.
...SKETA

LIVE A LIFE,
NOT AN
EXISTENCE.
...SKETA

DO THAT WHICH YOU ARE MOST AFRAID OF...

SKETA

DAILY ACTION AT YOUR CRAFT, BRINGS YOU CLOSER TO PERFECTION.

SKETA

Focus is Everything!

CARI
WORLD
RESPO

LIFE ROCKS!

...SKETA

ROME WASN'T BUILT IN A DAY, BUT IT WAS BUILT!

SKETA

Build y
realit

CHANGE NEEDS CHANGE.

...SKETA

Focus is Everything!

IF YOU CAN BEAT 'EM, JOIN 'EM; UNTIL AN OPPORTUNITY ARISES, WHEREBY YOU CAN TOSS 'EM.

...SKETA

IF YOU HA
JUST O

YOU H
DIF

# OUR
# YONE'S
# LITY.

## DOWNTIME IS EVERYTHING!
...SKETA

## Focus is Everything!

# CHANGE NEEDS CHANGE.
...SKETA

*reams a*
*ve in.*

## SUCCESS
## =
## HOW MUCH YOU WANT IT
## +
## HOW HARD YOU WILL WORK TO GET IT!
...SKETA

# LIFE ROCKS!
...SKETA

**PROVED,**
**SON'S**

**ADE A**
**CE.**

## Focus is Everything!

## EVERYDAY IS A BLESSED DAY.
...SKETA

# LIVE A LIFE, NOT AN EXISTENCE.
...SKETA

www.ingramcontent.com/pod-product-compliance
Lightning Source LLC
Chambersburg PA
CBHW041823090426

42811CB00010B/1093